In this series –

The Essential Rumi Readings
Rumi Readings for Achievement
Rumi Readings for Addiction
Rumi Readings for Careers & Work
Rumi Readings for College
Rumi Readings for Communication
Rumi Readings for Family
Rumi Readings for Grieving
Rumi Readings for Life
Rumi Readings for Love
Rumi Readings for Meditation
Rumi Readings for Mental Health
Rumi Readings for Mindfulness
Rumi Readings for Responsibility
Rumi Readings for Self-Esteem
Rumi Readings for Self-Healing
Rumi Readings for Sorrow & Joy
Rumi Readings for Youth

RUMI READINGS
FOR
MEDITATION

RUMI READINGS
FOR
MEDITATION

JALALUDDIN RUMI

The Scheherazade Foundation

The Scheherazade Foundation CIC
85 Great Portland Street
London
W1W 7LT
United Kingdom
www.SF.Charity
info@SF.Charity

First published by The Scheherazade Foundation CIC, 2025

RUMI READINGS FOR MEDITATION

© The Scheherazade Foundation

The Scheherazade Foundation asserts the right to be identified as the Author
of the Work in accordance with the Copyright, Designs and Patents Act 1988.

A CIP catalogue record for this title is available from the British Library.

ISBN 978-1-915311-75-7

Introduction

Jalaluddin Rumi was born in Balkh, Afghanistan, in the year 1207, and died in Konya, Turkey, in 1273.

During the sixty-six years spanning this pair of dates, he produced a range of extraordinary work in Persian which, today, is classed as 'Sufi Mysticism'.

In the seven and a half centuries since his death, Rumi's corpus, which includes *The Masnavi* and *Fihi Ma Fihi*, has been circulated widely across the Near East, the Arab world, and Central Asia.

Generations of students continue to commit selections of the 60,000 verses to heart, and allow Rumi's way of thought to permeate through all areas of their lives.

Although Orientalists venturing eastward from Europe in the 1700s occasionally made note of Sufi Mysticism, they tended to witness it through the more theatrical frills – such as 'whirling dervishes' – rather than through a deep appreciation of the texts.

It wasn't until the close of the nineteenth century that the first wholescale translations of Rumi's written work began to appear in Europe.

Even then, they remained very much the purview of a few academics, whose translations were – even for the time – laden with indescribably floral and cumbersome prose.

Although in the Occident, students would find themselves scrutinizing Rumi's corpus, it wasn't until more recently that accessible appreciations of his work became available.

A few years before his death, I asked my father – the Sufi scholar and thinker Idries Shah – for his thoughts on Rumi's legacy in the West.

Sitting in his favourite chair, a porcelain cup of green tea in hand, he looked at me hard.

'I never cease to be amazed,' he said.

'Amazed by what?'

'By the way people don't take what's perfectly packaged, and ready and waiting for them, but rather obsess with something else.'

'With what?'

'With endless and nonsensical trimmings, trappings, and paraphernalia.'

My father sipped his tea.

After a moment of silent thought, he continued:

'Read Rumi in the original Persian,' he said, 'and so delicate are the verses that you have tears rolling down your cheeks. Yet here in the West, it's served up as something submerged in a thick, glutinous gravy, so much so that its utterly inedible.'

I reminded my father that a series of publications had recently found their way to press – publications that presented Rumi's couplets in an utterly new way.

Stripped bare of what my father had referred to as 'gravy', they were light.

Indeed, they were lighter than light.

My father rolled his eyes at the thought.

'In any other place, and at any other time,' he said, 'people would be up in arms. Or, if they weren't, they'd be laughing until their sides split. Imagine it – Western poets with absolutely no knowledge of the original Persian text touting new, bestselling editions of Rumi's work! It's what we call "The Soup of the Soup of the Soup".'

In the years since my father's death, Occidental society has been flooded with all things Rumi.

Couplets ascribed to him are read solemnly at weddings across the United States, Europe, and beyond.

Wisdom drawn from his poetry is tattooed daily over the backs and limbs of Hollywood A-listers.

But the precious words uttered at weddings, tattooed into skin, and quoted in abundance, hold little or no bearing to the original verses of Jalaluddin Rumi.

So, there it is...

The great Sufi Master's wisdom available:

(a) in a form that's unreadable because it's all covered in glutinous gravy, or

(b) in another form that's completely distorted – the Soup of the Soup of the Soup.

One thing that *is* evident is that the West can benefit enormously from a clean, clear rendition of Rumi's thinking – as the East has done over the last seven hundred years.

For this reason, we have commissioned entirely new translations, gleaned in particular from *The Masnavi*. Selected and translated by native Persian-speaking scholars, the emphasis has been on maintaining the lightness of Rumi's poetry.

In an age of relentless speed and digital overload, and so as to allow the work to be accessed by those who may benefit from it most, we have arranged a series of bite-sized morsels by way of theme.

We encourage you to do what students, scholars, and ordinary people have done across the East for centuries...

To pick a single couplet, or a handful – and to read them over and over, allowing them to seed themselves in your mind.

Little by little, having taken root, they will blossom and bear fruit.

Tahir Shah

How to Use This Book

Rumi Readings for Meditation

This book is not meant to be read quickly.
It is meant to be returned to – like breath.
Like stillness. Like the quiet space between thoughts.

Rumi Readings for Meditation is a companion for your inner life.
A guide for those seeking calm.
A mirror for those walking the path of awareness.
A hand gently placed on the shoulder of those trying to listen more deeply – to themselves, to the silence, to something greater than the noise.

These one hundred quotes are drawn directly from *The Masnavi*, newly translated from the original Persian by The Scheherazade Foundation. They have been selected with care – to speak not only about meditation, but **from within it**.

- They are not instructions.
- They are not techniques.
- They are invitations.

Each one is a seed.
Let it fall into stillness, and see what grows.

Enter Quietly

You don't need to prepare anything to read this book.
But a moment of pause can help.

Try to read a single quote when you are not rushed.
In the morning before you begin.
At night before you sleep.
In the middle of the day, when the world spins too fast.

Read it once.
Then again.
Let the rhythm settle into you.

Close your eyes.
Notice what shifts – even slightly.

This is meditation.

A Book to Be Lived With

You do not need to read it in order.

You do not need to finish it.

You do not need to remember what you read.

Let the quotes accompany you, quietly.

As students across the East have done for centuries, return to one line again and again.

Let it become part of your breath.

The quotes are arranged in ten thematic parts. You may find yourself drawn to a specific part. Or you may open the book randomly.

Both are valid. Meditation begins where you are.

A Practice of Reading

After reading a quote, you might simply rest in its atmosphere.

Or you might ask yourself:

- What is being asked of me here?
- Where does this land in my body?

- What would it mean to live this line today?

There is no pressure to answer.

You may simply listen. You may journal. You may walk slowly with the words.

This is not a task – it's a return.

In Silence, in Company

You may wish to share this book in a meditation circle, a quiet moment with a friend, or in teaching.

You may read a quote aloud before a period of silence.

Let the words do their own work.

You don't need to explain them.

Often, they are more powerful when left unspoken after they've been heard.

No Need to Understand

Rumi often moves in metaphor.

Some quotes may seem obscure.

Some may land directly in the heart.

Others may make no sense at all – until months later, or not at all.

This, too, is part of the path.
Meditation is not about grasping – but about releasing.

Let each quote be what it is.
Let it open something quietly inside you.

This Book Is a Breath

Read one line.
Pause.
Breathe.

Rumi writes in this volume:
'This silence is like a great ship crossing the expansive ocean of Truth... As a sea-worthy vessel is needed for turbulent waters, so silence is required for self-expression in the depths of comprehension.'

Let the silence carry you.
Let the words dissolve into stillness.
Let the stillness say what words never can.

Part 1

Paths Leading to Inner Peace

1

By being vigilant and alert,
you will have the opportunity to observe
your actions in every single moment.

2

In the depths of thought and remembrance,
the mirror of the heart perceives unparalleled visions.

3

Declare the entitlements,
burn the lament of abomination,
adorn the iris of narcissus from this spectacle.

4

The one who has meticulously crafted it in seclusion,
has ultimately acquired the skill
from their cherished one as well.

5

When alone,
press your face against the door
and choose isolation,
even from your own Self.

6

What is the purpose of these exercises
performed by dervishes?
Those afflictions serve as a method
for preserving lives.

7

So the feast of lovers arrived,
listening to the *Sama'*,[1]
for in it lies the illusion of unity.

---

1   Dervish whirling to music, literally 'listening'.

8

When encountering quietude,
exercise caution:
misfortune befalls those
who do not possess inner tranquility.

9

It is appropriate to acquire knowledge
about hidden information,
as it has the power to reveal
what is concealed by spoken words.

10

From the outset,
you have a natural inclination towards prayer:
ultimately, you reward all prayers.

Part 2

Attaining Inner Serenity Through Prayer

11

Dear brother,
continue to pray, do not stop;
regardless of whether your request is granted or denied,
what truly matters?

12

Previously you said:
'Despite my knowledge of his personality,
he will promptly expose it,
based on your outward appearance.'

13

Lift your damaged hands in supplication:
God's grace will ascend towards the injured.

14

Those whose hearts are cleansed from suffering
can offer prayers that rise to the exalted Lord.

15

When I shed tears,
my compassion is awakened,
and those who shed tears experience the favour
I bestow upon them.

16

If you express deep sorrow and actively seek absolution,
the illumination concealed by divine favour will manifest.

17

The act of remembering the Divine
is considered pure
when purity is achieved.
At that point,
purity conceals itself,
and impurity disappears.

18

The world is like an ocean,
the body, a fish,
and the soul, like Jonah,
is hidden from the early morning light.
If the fisherman has enough skill,
the fish is released;
if not, it is engulfed and disappears.

19

When God wishes to help us,
He directs us towards prayer.

20

After this,
we will demand a great deal from you
to prevent the complete submergence of everything
in the foam of the sea.

Part 3

The Essence of
Serenity From Silence

21

An attentive listener
will appreciate profound and magnificent secrets,
like a lily
with its thousand messages unspoken.

22

The words contained within the breast
are the culmination of all intellectual thought.
When the mind is quietened,
it sees numerous facets of the inner Self.

23

Patience and stillness
act as conduits for the transmission of divine mercy.
To identify indications of divine kindness,
you must avoid engaging
in superfluous conversation
and trivial debate.

24

When love appears,
it leaves you speechless;
it does not create complication.
The being is hesitant to answer,
concerned that
a valuable gem may inadvertently be revealed.

25

When in the company of friends,
it is better to remain quiet
and not draw attention to yourself
within the circle.
Withdraw your outer layer into stillness,
and when searching for a signal,
do not becoming a signal yourself.

26

When faced with ignorance,
quietude is the appropriate response,
and is accompanied by a sense of calm.
Conversing with fools
is for the irrational.

27

This silence is like a great ship
crossing the expansive ocean of Truth.
As a sea-worthy vessel
is needed for turbulent waters,
so silence is required for self-expression
in the depths of comprehension.

28

Outward discourse is transient and fleeting,
like particles of dust.
Be quiet and attentive
for the needed time.

29

Stay silent to perceive the revelations of Truth,
as the murmurs of Truth hold immeasurable value,
like a hundred thousand lives in one.

30

I embody the strength and grandeur of a mountain,
and my words serve as the expression of my beloved.
I am a representation of a person,
and my visual depiction connects me
to that cherished someone.

Part 4
The Light of Truth in Seclusion

31

What depths does the wise one seek?
For in solitude lies the purity of the heart.
Why dwell in the darkness of the world
when you can avoid the pitfalls of society?

32

Embrace solitude
and choose seclusion
to prevent yourself
from being completely absorbed by the world.

33

He isolated himself,
then quickly advanced towards the sanctuary
where prayers were confirmed.
The truth was exposed for all to see,
leading to a natural increase
in awareness of consequence.

34

When alone,
whatever actions this body performs
are not done for the benefit of individuals of both sexes.
The combination of motion and calmness in isolation
is meant for nothing but Truth.

35

When there is absence of light
due to the deceitfulness of earthly companions,
seek solace in the cleansing benevolence
of the divine realm.
Interacting with others
might lead to moral decay,
prompting the desire to embark
on the journey of 'Oh Bilal,[2] let us depart!'

---

2   A companion of the Prophet Muhammad.

36

When I realized that martyrdom was not my fate,
I promptly pursued isolation and abstinence.
In the pursuit of self-improvement,
I embarked on a rigorous journey
to conquer my own inner demons,
subjecting my body to asceticism and fasting
to lessen my Self.
This withdrawal into seclusion was my greater *jihad*,
the intense personal struggle.

37

People seek solitude to avoid opponents,
not companions.
The focus is not on getting ready for winter,
but on preparing for the comforting presence of friends.

38

If you find yourself feeling hopeless
because you are alone,
find solace in the company of a dynamic partner,
like finding shade under the sun.
Look for a heavenly friend;
for when you do this,
God becomes your companion.

39

One who has dedicated themselves
to being alone eventually
gains knowledge from the presence of others.

40

Seeking refuge in pursuit of solace
will only bring misfortune
upon you from that direction.
Every corner has potential hazards and snares.
Peace can only be found
within the sanctuary of Truth.

Part 5

The Quality of Remembrance in Meditation

41

Externally, it is expressed as praise,
but internally, it is genuinely felt.
If spoken from the mouth,
it is merely a form of deception or enchantment.
Then God abruptly declares:
'I can perceive
both the inside and out.'

42

People frequently recite
the unadulterated appellation
without stopping.
This action is not fruitful
if it lacks genuine affection.

43

The Shah commanded us to invoke God.
Amidst the flames,
our vision found illumination.

44

Their chanting does not have the power to cleanse me;
Instead,
it is they who undergo purification and elevation.

45

It crushes ideas into a quivering:
recollection,
the radiant centre of this sombre creator.

46

Immerse yourself in the waters of remembrance
and forbearance to liberate yourself
from past ruminations and fixations.

47

Truth itself proclaims:
'O conceited one, lacking insight,
did you not gradually detach yourself
from my essence,
fragment by fragment?
If you had known about the mountain of Uhud[3]
that is within me,
you would have witnessed blood
spurting out from every rock.'

---

3   A mountain near Medina, site of a battle between the Prophet Muhammad
    and his enemies in 625 C.E.

48

As the soul establishes a connection with ultimate reality,
the act of recalling that reality
becomes the same
as recalling present reality.

49

Uttering the phrase 'Invoke Allah',
is not a behaviour exhibited by every dishonest person,
nor is it a response given by every deceitful individual.

50

If you abandon a regular practice in your spiritual journey,
you will experience the intense pain
and sharpness of losing
something of value.

Part 6

The Quality of Keeping Secrets in Meditation

51

If you encounter a vessel filled with dishonesty and lies,
stay silent and transform yourself into a vessel.
Avoid the enemy,
as it is fluid in nature.
Otherwise, your flask of knowledge would be shattered
by the stone of ignorance.

52

You asked:
'What information should be withheld by speech?'
There are no secrets hidden from the world.
Indeed, it is impossible
to articulate that particular instance
with someone who is inherently connected
to the fundamental nature of Adam's land.

53

Knowledge of the hidden
should only be given to one
able to articulate thoughts clearly.
A bird is not made to live beneath the sea.
Understand this,
for knowledge and Truth come only from God.

54

Placing cotton in the ear
reduces hearing.
Take off the blindfold.
The cotton within the ear
serves as the hidden element
transforming the outer ear into the inner ear.
Deprive yourself of sensory perception,
the ability to hear, and cognitive thinking,
in order to receive the message of 'Return'.

55

For someone who gains knowledge
of the mysteries of the celestial realm,
how insignificant are creatures of the world in comparison.
For one of heavenly behaviour,
what challenges does he encounter
while navigating the terrestrial realm?

56

Listen carefully to the silent,
as they may convey unspoken or unexpressed messages.
Listen intently to the sun's message,
which cannot be found in any written or spoken words.

57

O spirit,
surrender your heart entirely!
Through the cultivation of moral excellence
you will gradually reach understanding of hidden truths.

58

Within a perplexed heart devoted to God,
how can the enigma of the cosmos remain hidden?

59

The Source resides
in the hidden and extraordinary phenomena
concealed from those
who can only detect immediate effects.

60

O spirit burned by love,
you have transformed into something different.
O you who embrace the divine,
you are the divine and something beyond.
You comprehend the celestial mysteries
and the intricacies of various matters.
You read from the blank tablet,
and something beyond as well.

Part 7

The Quality of Music in Meditation

61

The aim of its music
does not reside in the sound produced by the lute,
but in the imagination of people
who long for that destination.
Only the reverberation of the celestial trumpet lingers,
while the lyre's sorrowful melody
and the drum's resounding thunder have ceased.
The resonance of each pleasant tune
evokes ancient agreement, and harmony.

62

The nightingale was enraptured by his own song;
one pleasure from his melody multiplied a hundred times.
His melodies embellished every meeting and assembly,
and through his music, they found rejuvenation.

63

The reed flute recounts the path marked by blood,
sharing stories of a love like Majnun's.[4]
This trail, its bloodstains,
is arduous, treacherous, and demanding.

---

4   A reference to the classic Middle Eastern love story Layla and Majnun.

64

The intensity of love is heightened by song,
like the flavour of a nut by a chestnut-seller's coals.

65

O flute,

how exquisite it is that you use what you know

to perform tasks driven from knowledge itself.

66

The meaning of the lute's message remains unknown,
arising from the combination of tearful emotions
and intense suffering within.
I experience detachment
between skin and flesh.
How can I express my sorrow and suffering
in this state of separation?

67

Unveil our true colour,

O cup-bearer,

within the untainted essence of wine;

merge us till both realms are freed from dishonour.

O cup-bearer, make haste!

Do you not see?

Our thoughts are sleepy with delay.

68

Has there ever been a time
when the insensitive
have appreciated the tune
produced by the harp and the lute?

69

O cup-bearer,
take advantage of the chance for joy and celebration!
Fill the cup with wine
from another goblet of wine.

70

Believers will tell you that
the creations of Paradise
have the power to convert any discordant sound
into pleasing ones.
All the elements of Adam
have been intricately intertwined
with those harmonies in Paradise.

Part 8

The Quality of *Sama'* in Meditation

71

Divine inspiration was bestowed on Moses
as God infused His spirit into him.
When Moses's radiance illuminates the mountain,
it causes the mountain to move.

72

Immersed in heavenly affection,
they transform into graceful performers,
exhibiting a flawlessness like the brilliance
of the full moon. They dance in synchrony
while their spirits ascend; do not ask how.
And those who contemplate their inner selves,
do not ask after them.

73

Dance where you break yourself;
remove the cotton from the beard of desires.

74

Not everyone possesses the necessary qualifications
to embark on the journey of genuine 'listening'.
Small birds do not rely on figs for their nourishment:
especially a bird of rotting carrion,
blind, and filled with delusion.

75

The divine nature and qualities
which maintained the unity of the universe
served as the adornment of His garment.

76

Permit me to give a few points
from the language of *Sama'*,
which has been represented
in a hundred elegant tongues.
You transcend both worlds –
this one and the one this dance embraces –
when you enter its domain.

77

For the sake of his soul, *Sama'* is restless.
What does this mean?
What is it waiting for?

78

O seekers, dance!
Spin, O little ones!
Our true King is king
in the kingdom of the world.
Tonight, among narcissi and roses,
with instruments in our hands,
our greatest possessions are tambourines and drums.

79

I once spied a dervish
heading toward the desert,
dancing and swirling
high in the air.
'In what ecstasy are you
so removed from worldly thoughts?'
I asked.
'Are you the bright sun or a new light?'
He answered:
'As soon as my feet were freed from their grasp,
my body felt light and my heart felt constricted.'

80

It acts as curtains without a platform,
strums strings in an amorphous manner.
There, reason and soul dance
to the regular beat of happiness and grief.
This breath holds that veil,
and we move like dancers on the paper of the pen.

Part 9

The Quality of Asceticism in Meditation

81

With great care, bend the curve of the Self,
for it is evil and does not aid righteousness.
Even when it is given generously,
one could get a hundred times more in return.

82

Keep your heart separate from desire
and refuse to give in to it,
for the opponent is the one you are fighting.
The condition won't be met,
and the outcome won't be avoided,
if you lack the endurance of patience.

83

Should abstinence come naturally to you,
take a bow and express gratitude,
O blessed one.
Thank the Almighty for bestowing
that austerity on you.
For He would have forced you by His order
if you had not accepted it voluntarily.

84

Remove the load
that the donkey is carrying;
take it now, to prevent any further harm.

85

The person who overcomes the tyranny of Self
can command the sun and the clouds.

86

When will the psychology of humans
grow more refined,
if not via action and asceticism?

87

So that you may understand
that freeing the soul from suffering
is the result of losing wealth and body,
make asceticism the purchase of your soul,
for you save your soul
when you commit your body to service.

88

Think of a human as an ugly, thick, untanned hide
that has retained some moisture.
To make it pure, delicate, and refined,
it needs rubbing, bitterness, and sharpness.

89

In asceticism,
suffering in this body is food for the soul;
death to the body is life.

90

O son,
you can instantly lift your head
from its concealed purity
if you wish to split open the robe.

Part 10

The Quality of Gratitude in Meditation

91

It is wise to express gratitude for gifts received,
lest everlasting anger come to you.
Observe this kindness and consider
who may be content merely to be grateful
for such plenty.

92

The wicked follow the path of obstinacy and ingratitude,
while the Prophet follows the path
of thanksgiving and gratitude.

93

The wicked are less faithful than dogs;
they will never show thanks.
Once a dog receives bread at the door,
it both returns to that door,
and prepares to be turned away.

94

Being grateful is uplifting;
compulsive gratitude is the rejection of one's gifts.
Gratitude gives you strength;
compulsion takes rewards away from you.

95

Gratitude leads to consciousness,
while blessings may cause unawareness.
Recall benefits under the authority of Truth
in the fold of thankfulness.

96

Those who continue in their laziness
without showing gratitude or patience
will eventually fall into the trap of compulsive behaviour.
These people will learn that
their lack of gratitude has led them
to become caught in a state of compulsiveness.

97

Thank goodness there are no more twists
and turns leading up to that point
when you make your escape.
He gives you a day free from snares
and fear of the enemy
when you thank Him.

98

Giving thanks to others
is really giving thanks to God,
since His grace permeates all charitable acts,
and His rights are inextricably linked
to what is morally correct.

99

In good times and bad,
I thank my friend because,
sometimes,
when faced with hardship,
nothing is worse than 'worse'.

100

Those who are ungrateful
are driven to the depths of fire
by their terrible ingratitude.

Finis

www.ingramcontent.com/pod-product-compliance
Lightning Source LLC
Chambersburg PA
CBHW020450100426
42813CB00031B/3320/J